The Grand Tour
My months of hitchhiking, biking and serving Her Royal Majesty

DAVE QUINTON

BOULDER PUBLICATIONS

Library and Archives Canada Cataloguing in Publication

Quinton, Dave, author
The grand tour : my months of hitchhiking, biking and
serving her royal majesty / Dave Quinton.

ISBN 978-1-927099-91-9 (softcover)

1. Quinton, Dave--Travel--Europe. 2. Europe--Description
and travel. I. Title.

D922.Q85 2017   914.04'555   C2017-904384-6

© 2017 Dave Quinton

Design and layout: Todd Manning
Cover illustration: Jessie Downey
Editor: Stephanie Porter
Copy editor: Iona Bulgin
Printed in Canada

Excerpts from this publication may be reproduced under licence from Access Copyright, or with the express written permission of Boulder Publications Ltd., or as permitted by law. All rights are otherwise reserved and no part of this publications may be reproduced, stored in a retrieval system, or transmitted in any form or by any means, electronic, mechanical, photocopying, scanning, recording, or otherwise, except as specifically authorized.

We acknowledge the financial support of the Government of Newfoundland and Labrador through the Department of Tourism, Culture and Recreation.

We acknowledge the financial support for our publishing program by the Government of Canada and the Department of Canadian Heritage through the Canada Book Fund.

To Bob

Contents

1. Across the Ocean 1

2. England, Part 1 13

3. Across the Channel 35

4. England, Part 2 79

5. Epilogue 101

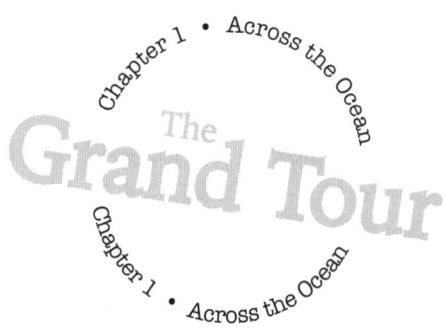

The Grand Tour

Chapter 1 • Across the Ocean

December 1, 1960

I was packing my duffle bag when the letter arrived. It was from northern Saskatchewan where my friend Don Poynter was teaching.

"Don't go to musty old Europe," he began. "You and Bob buy motorcycles and join me on a *real* adventure. We'll cycle from Hudson's Bay to Patagonia—through forest and jungle, over desert and pampa, from the Arctic to the Antarctic …" On and on Don rambled for 23 pages, begging Bob and me to join him on his madcap scheme.

Back then, in 1960, you couldn't even motor across Newfoundland. I doubted a Harley-Davidson could make it through the jungles of Brazil. Besides, how could I afford to buy a motorcycle?

I must admit to being tempted by his words. I was young and, after years of studying all winter and working lonely wilderness jobs all summer, I was filled with wanderlust, and

The Grand Tour

RESERVATIONS FOR:
STEAMSHIPS
AIRLINES
BUSLINES
HOTELS
SUMMER RESORTS
RAIL (BRITISH & CONTINENTAL)
AMERICAN EXPRESS TOURS
CARAVAN TOURS
THOMAS COOK & SON
DEAN & DAWSON TOURS
FRAMES TOURS
GLOBAL TOURS
LAMIN TOURS
MELIA TOURS
TREASURE TOURS
UNIVERSITY TOURS

"YOUR TRAVEL AGENT"

MARITIME TRAVEL SERVICE LTD.
76 GRANVILLE STREET
HALIFAX, N. S.

MEMBER

CABLE ADDRESS
"MARTRAV"

TELEPHONES
2-4441
2-4442
2-4443

October 11, 1960.

Mrs. J. Metherall,
SS #1 Site 4,
Bedford, N. S.

Dear Mrs. Metherall:

We are pleased to advise that we can offer the following accommodations for Mr. D. Quinton and Mr. R. Gray December 3, 1960:-

> "Nova Scotia", two berths in tourist class cabin 68 on C deck. This is a four berth inside room.

We are holding an option on this space which is due October 24th and we would appreciate being in receipt of a deposit of $30.00 per person to hold these accommodations on or before that date. The fare is $166.50 per person plus $1.00 each Canadian Port Tax.

Trusting that you will find this offer satisfactory, we remain,

Yours very truly,

MARITIME TRAVEL SERVICE LTD.

Sylvia M. Seymour

Roy Bowman,
Manager

SS/ps

---

the thought of roaring through the Wild West and on to South America was an exciting idea.

But so was hiking and bicycling through Europe. Don's letter had arrived too late, anyhow. Another college friend, Bob Gray, and I had already booked passage to England on the SS *Nova Scotia*. In fact, Bob was already en route

Stormy seas, a rough start to our adventure.

from Halifax. The passenger ship would soon dock here in St. John's. Who knew what adventures would await in England, Ireland, France, and Spain? We were committed to our Grand Tour.

I put away Don's letter and resumed packing.

Socks, shirts, underwear, scarf, overcoat? Well, winter was here … and it could be cold in England too. In went the scarf and overcoat (yes, even young men wore them in 1960). Skates? I didn't know—I never had been much of a hockey player on Mundy Pond.

Yet, everyone knew that the English were lousy hockey players. I could be a star over there! In went the skates.

Bob and I were on deck as the *Nova Scotia* steamed out the Narrows. We watched the muscular cliffs of Newfoundland become smaller and the ocean swell bigger and bigger.

It was cold. December, we discovered, was not the ideal month to cross the North Atlantic. But we stayed on deck as long as we could, watching the noddies* dance on the angry waves and wondering what adventures lay ahead.

The bitter wind finally drove us below deck. Our cabin was spartan compared with those in modern luxury liners, but we were delighted. For five years, from May until September, we'd lived and worked in the wilderness under canvas tents. To us, this was the Newfoundland Hotel.

We even had a porthole. This was a mixed blessing—in rough weather the sea swirled and gurgled angrily. And I confess it spooked me, just a little. It made me think of the opening scene in *Wuthering Heights*, where the ghostly Catherine scratches and calls at the window, "Let me in! Let me in!" I imagined drowned seamen peering in through that porthole.

I was queasy—me, a Newfoundlander, descended from sea dogs. Just imagine! And landlubber Bob, a mainlander, was lying on his bunk reading a book. Not a worry in the world.

"Bob!"

"What?"

"We're now in the spot where the *Titanic* went down."

"Oh." He kept on reading.

"Unsinkable. That's what they thought. Just think, 1,000 skeletons below us right now."

"Dave, shut up!"

---

* Seabirds, or fulmars.

Brief pause.

"Bob. What's that at the porthole?"

"What? I don't see anything!" He was slightly uneasy.

"Just my imagination, I suppose. Looked like a hand!"

Bob closed his book.

"Think I'll go back on deck … check the lifeboats … and get the latest iceberg report."

Bob's book hit the door as I scurried out.

On deck, in the fresh air, I felt better. And a little ashamed of myself, as I thought of my ancestors sailing across this same ocean hundreds of years before. No engines, no navigation aids. Just the wind and the stars. And at the end of the voyage, a wild untamed land. That took courage. I wondered if they had gotten seasick.

Maybe that's why they hadn't sailed back to England.

The dry heaves completely gone, I tried to encourage an elderly lady who was frightened to death. She kept rolling her eyes and rattling her prayer beads, convinced that the vessel was going to sink.

I wondered if Bob was still glancing at the porthole.

The wind picked up. The steward was trying to cheer up queasy passengers, saying we'd make record time with this wind. The old lady didn't give a damn. She was green. Rattle, rattle.

Down in the cabin, everything loose was sliding around on the floor. But, thank heavens, I'd finally gotten my sea legs. I figured I'd roll like a proper sailor when it was time to go ashore.

Bob had taken quite a tumble. When the vessel rolled, he had flown across the lounge and cracked his skull on the wall. The doctor who'd patched him up was loaded drunk. The first scar of our big adventure.

We decided it was time to discuss our finances. The tickets had cost me $166, Bob slightly more, as he'd boarded in Halifax. We had to keep enough to get back home. We had $700 or $800 each. Not much for a Grand Tour! (With 2017 prices in Europe, that would last two or three days, but this was 1960. We figured we'd be good for several months. Maybe.)

What odds? we'd go until our money ran out. Get jobs if we had to.

We were young and healthy. Footloose, and fancy-free. Living our dream.

The wind had abated and it was quite pleasant on deck as long as you were bundled up. We must have been about halfway across. Just imagine—the middle of the Atlantic, the cold grey North Atlantic.

I'd just finished reading *The Grey Seas Under*, by Nicholas Monserrat. It's about the battles of the North Atlantic in World War II. Bob and I talked about it while we were on deck.

We chatted with two English ladies who, like us, were gazing at the waves. Bob and I had been little fellows during the war and relatively safe in North America. These ladies had seen it all—the bombings, the aerial battles, the terror, the horror. They spoke of the wreckage of vessels and human remains scattered on the beaches. The war had ended

Eventually, calm seas prevailed.

15 years before but the memories were still vivid.

They invited us to visit them in Yorkshire. That was real nice of them—who says the English are cool and reserved?

The *Nova Scotia* and its twin ship, the *Newfoundland*, were passenger-cargo ships on regular runs across the Atlantic. From Boston they steamed to Halifax, then on to St. John's and across to Liverpool and back. That's how most people travelled to Europe in 1960. No glittering chandeliers or dance halls. No swimming pools or jewellery boutiques. And these ships weren't 10-storey-high floating skyscrapers/shopping malls filled with tourists.

There was gambling, though. One night I won $2 playing bingo and spent my windfall on a Wellington for Bob and me. Our first English brew.

We read. We talked and laughed; we chatted with other passengers. We gazed at the ocean and dreamed our dreams.

The *Nova Scotia*, from a brochure I picked up.

Just a gentle swell. The sun shining. All hands seemed to have their sea legs. The old lady who figured we were all doomed to Davy Jones's locker had put away her prayer beads and managed a smile.

Some female company. Fellow adventurers from the other side of the world—Joan from Australia and Liz from New Zealand. At night on deck, Bob and I showed off our knowledge of astronomy to the girls from Down Under. Liz and Joan were fascinated with the Big Dipper, the North Star, and the Milky Way. Guess the skies are different in Australia and New Zealand. We talked about going there. (Dream on!)

They joined us later in our cabin, where we shared oranges and candy. The girls got a kick out of being entertained by the last of the big spenders.

Liz (from New Zealand) and Joan (from Australia) on the deck of the *Nova Scotia*.

The smell of oranges made me think of travelling on the train for May 24th weekend, the "Trouter Special"—oranges and wet socks and beer. And Dad's big basket full of pink trout. There I was with two beautiful girls and I was thinking of trout and wet socks. Was I completely nuts?

"A table richly spread in regal mode, with dishes piled, and meats of noblest sort and savour," as Milton wrote. Our last dinner on the *Nova Scotia*, a farewell dinner they called it. What a feast! Nobody would believe the grub we put away. Henry VIII didn't have it any better, and Bob and I stuffed ourselves. We doubted if we'd eat like that for a while. Bob had the steward sign his menu to testify to what he'd eaten.

The Grand Tour

> "A table richly spread in regal modes, with dishes piled,
> and meats of noblest sort and savour" — Milton

Hors d'Oeuvres

Chilled Melon

Table Celery — Chilled Grapefruit

Consommé Paysanne — Cream of Celery

Fillets of Sole with Lemon

Poached Turbot, Duglere

Buttered Spaghetti & Tomato

Creamed Sweetbreads & Mushrooms

Ham & Beef Croquettes, Bercy

Roast Vermont Turkey, Cranberry Jelly
Giblet Gravy

Garden Peas au Beurre — Cauliflower au Gratin

Potatoes: Roast Boiled Creamed

Cold Buffet

Salami Sausage Boiled Ham Silverside of Beef

Lettuce & Tomato Salad
Dressings: French & Vinaigrette

Peach Melba

Olde English Plum Pudding, Rum Sauce

Trifle Anglaise

Ice Cream with Wafers

Cheese

Cream Danish Blue Cheshire

Fresh Fruit Figs Dates Mixed Nuts

Coffee Rolls

The menu for our final feast.

A seven-day voyage with three meals a day and a splendid farewell feast, for $166? A bargain, even by 1960 standards.

After the feast, we staggered up on deck where we chatted with Ronnie Lambert, a physiotherapist on her way home after working at a hospital in St. John's. She pointed out the lighthouse in Cork.

We'd made it across! Our first glimpse of the Old World!

An air of excitement built on the *Nova Scotia*. There was music and dancing. Some crazy guy threw his cap overboard. The old seasick lady winked at me. Bob laughed at me. Through the Irish Sea we sailed. Past Angelsey in Wales. A few more hours and we'd be in Liverpool. Our adventure was about to begin.

Chapter 2 • England, Part 1
The Grand Tour

A huge, grey city sprawled before us, smothered in mist. Or was it smog? Mid-afternoon and already it was getting dark. Of course, Liverpool is farther north than St. John's, so the sun sets a little later. And the shortest day of the year was rapidly approaching.

It was our first glimpse of England. The Old Country, as my people called it. The Quintons, in fact most Newfoundland families, came from here hundreds of years ago. Well, the vast majority came from southwestern England—the West Country, it's called today. Surely some came from Liverpool. I didn't know.

In fact, I didn't know much about this place. Where do we go? What were we to do with our small mountain of luggage?

A porter snapped us out of our stupor. He grabbed our luggage and dumped it in his cart and took off. We chased him like two puppy dogs through the bustling crowds. He dumped our stuff on the curb and stood like a statue. "A tip," Bob whispered frantically. I fumbled through a pocketful of unfamiliar British currency and plopped a large coin in his great palm.

He stared at it. And stared.

I got the point and timidly added another coin—a thicker one. It transformed the man. He grinned, doffed his cap, thanked me, and called me "guv'nor."

In England just a few minutes and I had a title. What an amazing place.

I wondered how much I had tipped him.

A taxi screeched to a halt. The vehicle was square, big, black, and tall. I was sure you could walk in wearing a top hat. We piled our bags and suitcases on board and zoomed through the busy streets of Liverpool, mouths agape. It wasn't Water Street! Huge stone buildings, bobbies directing traffic, girls in short skirts, a towering statue of Nelson (I believe), girls in short skirts, bustle, bustle, everyone in a hurry, double-decker buses, girls in short skirts …

Our taxi pulled up in front of a railway station. Out with the luggage.

"Bob," I whispered, "your turn to tip."

He hesitated, then deposited a coin in the cabbie's palm. The cabbie gazed at it for a moment. Quietly he got aboard, started up, and, as he pulled away, he screwed down the window and flipped the tip to us.

"'Ere, mates. Buy yourselves a slice of bread!"

We looked at each other and laughed. We'd have to take a crash course in British currency. What complicated money! Guineas, crowns, shillings, tuppance, thruppence, bobs, ha'pennies. And people here argued that was easier than the metric system. "Oh well, at least we got titles," Bob said. "I'm a mate and you're a guv'nor."

Our plan was to send our luggage by rail to London and hitchhike there so that we could see some of the English countryside. We'd collect our luggage after we'd found a place to stay in London.

We chatted with two girls in front of us in the lineup for the railway ticket window. Since they were going to London, they offered to check our luggage on their tickets. They said it would save us "a heap."

So that's what we did, hiding away as the girls purchased tickets, lest the agent got suspicious. It worked. While waiting for the train, we treated our new friends to a coffee. They got a real kick out of being "picked up" on Lime Street, Liverpool's rather notorious red light district. Bob, who was quite knowledgeable about music, knew a "skittle song" about Maggie who once prowled Lime Street. He sang a verse ...

Oh Maggie Maggie May, they have
taken you away and you'll never
walk down Lime Street anymore

The girls laughed at this crazy Canadian singing a skittle song.

Bob continued to amaze me. Where had he picked that up? Our English girlfriends told us that skittle songs were old-fashioned. The young crowd in Liverpool liked the Silver Beatles music better. Had we ever heard of Paul McCartney and Ringo Starr? We hadn't. (It was 1960, after all.) They had heard of a young Elvis Presley, though, from our side of the Atlantic.

Then 'twas time for them to catch the train … and our luggage on their tickets.

"Dave, did you copy down their names and addresses?" Bob asked, as the train chugged out of the station and we waved goodbye to our girlfriends and our worldly possessions.

"No, I thought you did."

We looked at each other. Two gullible hicks on their Grand Tour.

England, December 1960. Not the best time to hitchhike.

"Oh well, we've got our packsacks." I wondered if my skates would end up in a pawn shop.

Liverpool is a major shipping and industrial port, one of the largest cities in England, a prime target for German bombers in World War II. We didn't see much sign of the damage they had inflicted, though. I supposed the city had recovered and rebuilt. Thousands had been killed. and many children had been sent to relative safety in rural Wales not far away.

It was hard to believe that we were in England, with Scotland just to the north, Ireland a ferry ride away, and France a few hundred miles to the south—then Spain, Italy, and a smorgasbord of other countries. Back home in Newfoundland, you couldn't even drive or cycle from St. John's to Gander. Here there were roads everywhere, and trains.

We walked for a while. After we got tired, we boarded a bus—a great way to see a big city. We noticed that everyone drove on the "wrong" side of the road (we were later told that cars burned petrol, not gasoline).

An aristocratic elderly lady seated next to me was quite chatty, much to my surprise (I still thought the English were going to be quite reserved). She must have figured that we were from "the colonies," given our garb and accents. And, I suppose, given the way our eyes were riveted on the passing scenes. She informed me that a bus is not a bus; it's a coach. A truck is a lorry. And a trunk in a car is a boot.

What do you put on your feet in the winter? I wondered. But I didn't want to be saucy.

"Look at the movie that's playing," blurted Bob.

"It's not a movie. It's a film," she corrected.

We'll have to learn the English language all over again, we decided.

It wasn't just a new vocabulary that we had to learn. It was the accent, the pronunciation. In North America, the letter *r* is hard. You hear it (except in Boston and, for some reason, in Port de Grave). In England the *r* is soft. In fact, it disappears completely. Heart sounds like *hawt*; park like *pawk*.

I hadn't been to the West Country yet but I had been told that they do pronounce their *r*'s there. Since that's where most the Quintons came from, I guess we inherited it. And of course those of us of Irish descent pronounce the hard *r* too. (Quinton, you should be a linguist.)

The night before this coach ride we had been invited for a meal at the home of Ronnie Lambert, the physiotherapist we had met on the boat, outside Liverpool. We were enjoying the meal, chatting away with our hosts, when the conversation turned to the bottling of preserves. Mr. Lambert mentioned "jars of jam." He of course pronounced it in the English way. It sounded to Bob like *jaws* of jam. Figuring he was on to some unique English custom or way of preserving fruit, Bob blurted out, to my horror: "*Jaw* of jam! What's a *jaw* of jam? Haven't heard of that before!"

Stunned silence, except for a subdued yelp from Bob as I kicked his shin under the table. He quickly grasped his faux pas. We both turned red, and Bob sputtered an apology. Everybody laughed heartily, god bless 'em. Bob had a bruise on his shin.

Two young fellows on their big freedom trip, visiting a cathedral? Yes, and I must say it was an awesome sight. The steeple was lost in the mist, towering to heaven, I suppose. How in the world did people build such huge structures hundreds of years ago, without cranes and life insurance policies? Well, they say Newfoundlanders built the skyscrapers in New York. The Liverpool clergy must have imported a construction crew from Conception Bay!

We crept around inside, marvelling at the incredible workmanship.

When it was time to go, we discovered we'd been locked in. Couldn't get the door open. Imprisoned in an English cathedral!

Our halloos echoed through the cathedral and finally, out of nowhere, a warden appeared. We explained that we'd been so fascinated that we'd lost all track of time. Delighted that two colonials were so interested, the warden took us on a tour and answered our questions.

"Yes, the cathedral is large. In fact, it's the largest in Britain, some say the largest in Europe. The spire towers 500 feet above the river Mersey.

"The pipe organ is the largest in the world too," he bragged. "10,000 pipes. The peal bells weigh 31 tons ... Look at the chandeliers. They're 170 feet above the floor and weigh a ton each. It takes five men all day to change a light bulb!"

This sounded too much like a Newfie joke to me, but I kept my mouth shut. (Many years later I discovered that a local boy named Paul McCartney had failed in his audition for the choir in this cathedral.)

Time to go. The warden let us out of the cathedral and we resumed our stroll through old Liverpool. Fine dining that night: bangers and mash (sausages and mashed potatoes). It was delicious. I couldn't wait to try bubble and squeak ... the English language was getting more and more complicated for us. But then, I supposed, no one in Liverpool knew what fish and brewis was.

Bob had an International Youth Hostel book, which saved us a heap, as our girlfriends (the ones with our luggage) would say. Youth hostels were scattered all over Europe and were a wonderful way for young people with limited means (and that was us) to see the world.

Bob's youth hostel book. For one or two dollars a night (and a chore in the morning), we had our choice of places to stay.

Bob was the navigator and planner. He'd read voraciously and mapped out our route. I was content to coast along. So far, so good.

After a huge breakfast of porridge, bacon, and eggs, we did our chores, as was the custom in youth hostels. In exchange for the ridiculously low rates, we were expected to pitch in and work for a while.

We lugged coal with the help of our mischievous seven-year-old supervisor.

Then we had ploughman's lunch (meat, pickle, cheese, and bread) in a pub.

They're wonderful places, these pubs. Not at all like the beer taverns back home in Newfoundland. Oh, they served beer, of course. Most of it on tap, flat and warm. But there was so much more than beer. You could eat a meal at a reasonable price, read a newspaper, play darts, chat. The pub was (and is) a social institution.

When it was closing time, the publican (bartender) shouted out, "Time gentlemen please." All hands (ladies as well as gentlemen) downed their drinks and quietly paraded out. Very civilized. No rackets at all, not like some garden parties I'd been to at home.

Hitchhiking was nothing new to Bob and me. We'd thumbed our way around the Maritimes and New England many times while we were at college. Now it was time to hit the road for some serious thumbing in England.

A lorry driver picked us up, and gave us some advice on how to hitch a ride. First thing, he said, get rid of our scarves. Although they were in fashion in North America, scarves apparently weren't part of a hitchhiker's garb in England. Something to do with the class system, I suppose.

So, though it was damp and chilly, we dumped our scarves. The lorry drive took us to the medieval city of Chester. Now this was the kind of England I'd expected. Surrounded by a huge stone wall built by the Saxons (or was it Romans?) to keep out the wild Celtic Welshmen. Inside, half-timbered houses and shops and a forest of crooked chimneys.

Hungry, we wandered into a cozy pub, our refuge from the chill of the road. A wood fire blazed in the hearth and, of all people, Hank Williams was warbling in the background.

Bob and I looked at each other. Hank Williams? Here in merrie olde England? We had to ask the publican why he wasn't playing "Greensleeves" (written, they say, by Henry VIII) or "Land of Hope and Glory"?

Turned out the publican was simply a fan. Loved all Hank's heart-wrenching songs. Photos of Hank were plastered all over the walls along with, of all things, shots of the RCMP Musical Ride. Apparently they'd performed near Chester a few years before.

A country and western singer and Mounties on horseback in the heart of Old England! We ordered a meal and soon two beautiful girls appeared carrying steaming plates of steak and kidney pie and two pints of bitter.

And so, warmed by the log fire, serenaded by Hank Williams, Bob and I dug into the most scrumptious of En-

Chester, a view from the wall.

glish meals. Could it get any better than this? Musty old Europe, indeed.

After roaming through Chester and walking around the city on its ancient walls, we decided we'd better search for a hostel. It was cold and damp and getting dark.

A bus (oops—*coach*) carried us to the vicinity of the hostel. Supposedly. But it was a long tramp through deserted streets. It was pitch black. We followed a treed driveway, expecting a headless horseman to gallop by at any minute.

A spooky mansion loomed ahead, quiet as a tomb. A dog howled in the distance. The Hound of the Baskervilles? A faint light glimmered through a window, and I lit a match. Yes, it was the right place—the youth hostel.

We knocked and stepped back. After a long while the door creaked open. A 40ish redhead quietly ushered us in.

"Yes, this is the hostel," she said, "and yes, we have a room. In fact, you're the only guests." Then, after a pause, "Only the mad ones come here." She laughed.

Bob and I glanced at each other as we were led past a row of huge empty rooms to our military-style cots.

With a mysterious smile, our hostess bade us good night. As we crawled into our cots, we heard an eerie cackle.

"Rochester's wife!" I whisper to Bob. "Where's the fire extinguisher?"

Dave. Shut up!

All thoughts of Jane Eyre had disappeared in the morning. Sunny skies, a huge breakfast, and warm, chatty hostel keepers. Now, this was a great way to travel.

The lorry drivers were kind to us vagabonds. The next ride took us to Wales, a small diversion.

It was nearly dark when we were dropped off in a village with an impossible name that I forgot to copy down in my journal. The hills were haloed in mist. We could hear sheep bleating in the distance.

Finally, the hostel sign! An old gentleman ushered us into a mansion. Nothing like this back home in St. John's—certainly not in my part of town. Circular Road or Waterford Bridge Road, maybe. It was ornately furnished, with a log fire crackling in a monstrous fireplace. The place must have been hundreds of years old. I was certain some lord or duke had lived here.

And so, visiting royalty Lord Quinton and Lord Gray dried their wet vamps by the blazing hearth while they sipped mugs of cocoa. It was great.

"Bob, I wonder where Don Poynter is now?"

"Probably stuck in a snowdrift on the prairies."

I read a book about Wales while we sat in front of the fire. An interesting place. Home of the ancient Celts, who were forced out of England by the invading Saxons over 2,000 years ago. Wales is now part of the United Kingdom, of course, but the Welsh are fiercely proud of their culture and heritage.

Welsh is still spoken by some, especially in the north. I knew that much, as my Aunt Jessie is married to a Welshman. Uncle Bill Morgan is fluent in the old language; it's got to be one of the most difficult in the world to learn—and spell. (How would you like to live in a place called Llanfairpwllgwyngyllgogerychwyrndrobwyll-llantysiliogogogoch?)

Although the vast majority of Newfoundlanders are of English and Irish descent, there are a great many Welsh names back home too: Morgan, Jones, Evans, Roberts, Edwards ... maybe there is more Welsh blood in us than we think.

Socks dry, it was time to hit the sack. Or, I should have said, time to retire to my bedchamber.

I was getting to like this flat English beer. Over a bitter, I watched four old-timers playing snooker in a pub. They must have been in their 80s—red-faced Jack with a vest stretched over his potbelly. Hawk-nosed Peter, whose eyes never wandered from the table, even with a tankard to his mouth. And long, lanky 'arry with the salt and pepper cap, and the old colonel with the curved pipe.

The crowd egged them on, but not a peep from the combatants. Serious stuff, this snooker.

In a corner, an old lady with a sleeping dog at her feet was reading a newspaper and having a toddy. A fire was crackling in the fireplace. The crowd was encouraging 'arry, about to make a crucial shot, concentrating. Nobody was watching me. Thought I'd try a sketch of 'arry and his mates.

London.

We're here—the biggest city in the world. (Well, that's what my school books had told me, though Singapore and Mexico City are far bigger in the 21st century.)

But London! The heart of the British Empire. Buckingham Palace. The Queen. Big Ben. Tower of London. Winston Churchill. Charles Dickens. Oliver Twist.

We entered a pub called Dirty Dicks. The patrons told me to push a button and a mad, very realistic, cat suddenly screeched across the ceiling, frightening the life out of me. Crazy sense of humour, those cockneys.

We picked up our luggage. Those Liverpool girls weren't crooks after all.

Where were we going to stay? We found what must have been the cheapest place in London. We met Bluey, a New Zealand seaman who'd been staying there a long time.

He was trying to get a berth on a ship headed back home, or at least somewhere south to escape the damp and cold.

Bluey, what a character—his money was running out, yet he was always smiling, joking, and forever looking for big English pennies to feed the miserable heater. Needless to say, there was no central heating in this posh establishment. It might have been that, or the weather, or because I'd thrown away my scarf, but whatever the reason, I caught a dilly of a cold in London.

What a way to spend my first Christmas away from home. No tree, no presents. No turkey dinner. All stuffed up and miserable with Bluey squeezing pennies into a machine, as we warded off the damp and cold. I thought of Don, probably in hot Mexico.

Bob finally convinced me to go to a clinic. There I was examined by an Indian doctor wearing a colourful sari. She wasn't sure if a Canadian qualified for medical assistance, but she took pity on a fellow colonial, I suppose, and treated me.

A day or two later I was as good as new. Thanks, Doc!

It was time to leave soggy England. Like Bluey, we longed for a warmer, drier climate. We decided to head south—after we had visited Westminster Abbey.

I wanted to see the ancient abbey. I'd heard so much about it. William the Conquerer was crowned there nearly 1,000 years ago. Kings, queens, poets, scholars, and, I suppose, a few rogues are entombed there—a pageant of my people's history.

Bob, with his passion for music, wanted to hear a famous countertenor, who was singing in the choir. I'd never hear of Alfred Dellor and didn't know what a countertenor was, but I would soon find out.

We found seats next to the choir. In fact, we were practically *with* the choir. Bob had his mini tape recorder and recorded Mr. Dellor's singing. An amazing, high-pitched voice.

When the choir paraded out, the countertenor in his robes passed right by us and spotted the tape recorder. He paused dramatically and gave Bob a withering look. We shrunk in our seats and scurried away as fast as we could.

We purchased two second-hand bicycles. Mine was a Triumph 79118 and Bob's a Swift 72788. We found a place to store most of our luggage and loaded up our bikes with the essentials. Our survival gear included a pup tent, a Primus stove, a change of clothes, a bar of soap, two towels, assorted pots, maps, Bob's hostel book, a flashlight, passports and wallets, pencils, notebooks, and a few chocolate bars.

We must have been quite a sight, winding our way through the London traffic, dressed in our drab anoraks, with all our gear strapped on the parcel carriers or dangling from the handlebars as we set out on the next leg of our grand adventure. Tally most frightfully ho!

We had planned to be gone for four or five months, maybe longer. Two gypsies. Two happy wanderers.

We didn't get very far on our first day. Holed up in a hostel. Then it was on to Canterbury.

Pausing by a thatched-roof cottage, en route to Dover—my first day on my ancient bicycle.

Another place steeped in history. It was amazing to think Canterbury had been a Celtic city 2,000 or more years ago. Then the Romans had taken over, followed by the Danish Vikings, the Saxons, the Normans. Then there's the Canterbury Tales, murder of Thomas Becket, and on and on.

"Bob, look—the tomb of King Henry IV!" I'd read about him in school. Here was my chance to impress Bob, an English major.

"Once more into the breach, dear friends, once more. Or close the wall up with our English dead," I dramatically stated.

"That's *Henry V*." Bob rolled his eyes.

I needed something to read, because once we crossed the channel I supposed it would be hard to find anything written in English. The Chaucer Bookshop of number 6 Beer Cart Lane (great address!) was stuffed with what must have been a million books stacked in apparent chaos. I figured the owlish owner perched on a stool reading a book in the corner knew where to find every title.

He peered over his glasses when I asked if he had any books about Newfoundland. No, he didn't, but he promised to contact me if he should happen to get any. Would I leave my address?

I explained that I was a travelling man at the time, so I gave him Dad's address back home. I supposed it was unlikely I'd ever hear from him, but who knew?* Mr. Jarvis, the owner, told me that a man called Joey Smallwood had been purchasing a lot of Newfoundlandia in England.

---

* A year later, back in Newfoundland, came a letter from Mr. Jarvis informing me he had acquired a copy of John Guille Millais's *Newfoundland and Its Untrodden Ways*. It was the author's copy. Apparently Millais's widow had sold all the books in her husband's library, and I could have it for £2. An original Millais sells for about $400 in 2017, the author's copy probably more. But the book is worth more than money. It's a real treasure, a reminder of my trip abroad and the cluttered bookstore on Beer Cart Lane.

But why was I looking for Newfoundland books? It was my European adventure—was I really that homesick? I bought a novel, but I tired of it quickly.

A night's sleep and then we were off to Dover.

Somewhere between Canterbury and Dover, Bob's handlebar suddenly twisted around, throwing him off and through a hawthorn hedge. A nasty tumble, yet I couldn't help but laugh as he emerged from the bushes, looking like he'd been clawed by a cat.

It inspired me to compose the following ballad:

Oh Robert the bicycle rover
Flew through a thorn bush near Dover
It was quite a thump
On his head was a lump
And his face scratched a thousand times over.

I did take some poetic licence: Bob wasn't hurt. A turn of the wrench and the handlebar was fixed and on we sped to Dover.

"(There'll be bluebirds over) the white cliffs of Dover," as the song goes, but it was a grey mauzy day when Bob and I cycled into town and searched for a place to stay. From the hostel window the cliffs weren't exactly white, and I patiently waited with my camera for a bluebird to appear.

Here's the best I could do: a lonely gull, staring at me.

Guess the bluebirds were migrating south, like us.

Next day we were to cross the English Channel. The French call it La Manche, the Sleeve. Bob told me that. I don't know a word of French.

Chapter 3 • Across the Channel
The Grand Tour

Boulogne, France. We had arrived on the continent of Europe. It was exciting to be in a foreign country. England was foreign, of course, but the language is basically our own. It's something to be suddenly immersed in a tongue you can't understand at all.

Bob had taken French in school, so he could, with some sign language, manage to converse. But the foreign language I was taught in school was Latin. Latin! Imagine. My teachers must have been training me to be a Roman centurion. I was lost.

We cycled southward but we discovered that northern France could be quite cold in January. Not so bad in the youth hostels, but our little pup tent was not the warmest place in the world. Thank heaven for our sleeping bags, cheap though they were. We usually cycled 10 miles or so after we had gotten up, just to get warm, while keeping our eyes open for a little café, hoping to reach one before our knuckles turned blue.

Breakfast was simple: coffee with bread and jam. The jam was served loose in a dish, not in the stupid little plastic containers used in Barneys or the Candlelight restaurants back home.

Very civilized, the French.

And the bread. *Ohh la la*, as the French would say, though I hadn't yet heard it uttered.

The loaves were about 3 feet long. Horsing around with Bob, I presented arms with the loaf, pretending it was a rifle. We heard a laugh. A bunch of Frenchmen had been watching me from a window. Crazy Canadians.

Bob told me that my rifle wasn't a loaf; it's a bag-et, or something. Long and skinny, and wonderfully tasty. We'd see little kids running home with a loaf from the bakery in the morning, which made me think of us boys lined up at the back of Mammy's Bakery back home. Ten cents for a big bag of trimmings from the apricot squares and raisin squares (sinkers, we called them, because they were so heavy).

On our way southward, we arrived in Amiens. This place suffered terribly from the bombings in the war. And the trenches, where millions of Allied and German soldiers had been killed. Yes, millions. And countless civilians, men, women, and children. Unbelievable.

We wandered through the great cathedral that had miraculously escaped the bombs. I was startled to see on a pillar, in English, a plaque in memory of the Newfoundland soldiers who had fought and died nearby:

A plaque honouring the Newfoundland Regiment is on display in the cathedral in Amiens.

> TO THE GLORY OF GOD, TO THE HONOUR OF THE ISLAND AND TO THE ENDURING MEMORY OF THOSE OF THE NEWFOUNDLAND CONTINGENT WHO FELL IN THE FIRST BATTLE OF THE SOMME.
>
> BEHOLD, THIS STONE SHALL BE A WITNESS TO US.

We didn't realize it at the time, but we were close to the Somme River. Uncle Herman and Uncle Will were on the front lines here and cousin Gus was fatally wounded. He was only 19, younger than me.

It was cold cycling through northern France in January. At night we slept in our pup tent, once in an old deserted barn. We cooked our meals on our tiny stove. We were exploring old Europe, living our dream. Not once did we regret our decision to be exactly where we were. We laughed a lot.

Bob, half-frozen, as we approached Paris, January 1961.

I took a photo of Bob as we neared Paris. Ancient bikes, loaded down, half frozen to death ... and happy.

After we found a youth hostel, we proceeded to explore Paris, the city of light, the epitome of culture and sophistication. For centuries a magnet for poets and writers and philosophers—and now it had to put up with us.

How are they gonna keep me back on the rock after I've seen Paree?

Bob, in his best, in Paris.

We saw the Eiffel Tower and, culture vultures that we were, visited the Mona Lisa in the Louvre. I planned to brag about this to my artist friend Gary when I got back home.

With a motley crowd of young people from France, Italy, and Rhodesia, we laughed and danced and shared a bottle of wine in an inexpensive little café off the beaten track. *Vive la France!* (Yes, I'm showing off.)

Clara, the Italian girl, said something strange. Normally boisterous, bubbly, and full of fun, she became strangely quiet, as she said, "David, you and Bob are soft, aren't you?"

Soft? We were in great shape, in the prime of our lives—hiking, cycling, and roughing it, on a restricted diet. What was she talking about? I didn't know how to respond, but then it was more of an observation than a question. But it got me thinking.

At about our age, Clara would have been a child in war-torn Italy, while life for us in Canada was peaceful, easy. We played cowboys and Indians, while kids in Italy were barely surviving. At university, I once complained to my lab mate about the smell of formaldehyde on my fingers after we had dissected a pickled cat in zoology lab. Kris, a student from Germany, had overheard and said, "David. Do not complain. I had to hunt cats to eat during the war." I stopped complaining.

I wondered if Clara meant innocent, not soft. Anyway, she was soon herself, laughing and joking.

Paris was exciting, but we couldn't stay forever. The

Mediterranean, and warm weather, beckoned. But France is a big country, and we decided to put our bikes and us on a southward-bound train for a while. Skip over the heart of the land. It *was* winter.

So we got on a train and chugged through the centre of France on our way southward to where it was warm. It seemed crazy to be freezing on our bikes when we could be cycling along the sunny Mediterranean coast. We both wanted to get to Spain eventually—there was so much we wanted to see!

The Loire Valley. It was the first time I'd been warm in weeks. I felt like Sam McGee from Tennessee. It was hard to believe it was nearing the end of January. I wondered if Bluey was still sticking pennies in the heater back in London. He'd love it along the Loire, a giant river that starts somewhere in the Alps and flows all the way to the Mediterranean. We cycled through towns and villages and orchards and farms. Beautiful country.

Bob kept singing in French about a place called Avignon. Sir-le-pon Avignon or something. We'd soon be there, wherever it was.

It was getting warmer! Back home, Dad and my brother Don would have the storm windows on and a blaze in the fireplace. Or maybe they were out fishing through the ice.

Orange trees.

Avignon—finally, the place Bob had been singing about non-stop. I was surprised to learn that Avignon was the seat of the Roman Catholic church back in the 14th century. A bunch of popes lived here instead of in Rome. Not sure why! I thought I might get a chance to practice my Latin.

"*Amo amas amat. Ceasar adsum iam. Pompei ad erat.*" (Translation: Caesar has some jam for tea, Pompei had a rat … I failed Latin in Grade 11. Bill Rompkey and I had to study it from Miss Carmichael in order to enter Memorial University in 1953.)

We cycled south from Avignon and there it was—the

blue Mediterranean. Gentle breezes blowing in from Africa. A few hundred miles to the east is Italy and then Yugoslavia, Czechoslovakia, Greece, Turkey, and the Holy Lands. This sea is the cradle of civilization. People had been writing poetry and painting and building palaces here when my ancestors back in England were painting themselves blue and throwing rocks at each other.

We cycled past towns perched on hillsides. Houses built of stone. We saw olive trees and other trees I didn't recognize. Some trees looked ancient. My forestry courses weren't much good to me here; it was another world. Lots of grapes here, though, and wine.

Old and twisted trees along the road.

The Grand Tour

In Sete we found the closest thing we'd seen to an English pub since we had left England. Two large, buxom women were singing as they played cards with three men. The oldest fellow reminded me of 'arry in England, but far noisier, with an insane, cackling laugh. He said something to one of the women and she raised her elbow to him. I didn't know what it was all about, but everyone sure seemed happy. Everyone was singing, even the bartender as he polished glasses.

One woman, red in the face, triumphantly slapped her cards on the table. A roar from the others. She must have gone 30 for 60 and made it!

Tired, sweaty, and hungry after a hard day of cycling, Bob and I pressed our noses against the window of a fancy restaurant.

"Bob, look," I groaned.

"Food, glorious food. I'm starved."

"I'm famished. Sure, we haven't eaten all day."

"Too bad we can't go in. It'll cost a fortune."

"Yeah, and everyone is dressed up."

"We look like a couple of smelly hobos."

"Let's go around the block and find a cheaper place or a grocery store. Get a hunk of cheese or some bully beef. Do the French eat bully beef?"

"Thought you'd be looking for fish and brewis."

Around the corner we cycled, and sure enough there was a humble grocery store. Bob, in his halting French, explained that we wanted to buy some food.

"Wee, wee, mon sewer," the grocer responded and enthusiastically ushered us to a door and a passageway.

"Bob, what's goin' on?" I whispered. "Where's he takin' us?"

He shrugged.

Then the grocer opened another door and, with a grand flourish, waved us in.

"Voila, messiers!"

Yikes! We were in the same fancy restaurant we'd peered into a few minutes before. You could probably still see the imprint of our noses on the window.

As we stammered something in Fringlish, the maître d' swooped over and hustled us to a table, rattled off something in French and left us gazing at the menu, dumbfounded.

We peeped at the other patrons. Nobody seemed to look down their aristocratic noses at us. Though elegantly dressed, they barely noticed the two foreign vagabonds in their midst.

We looked at each other and laughed.

An incredibly tall waiter suddenly stared down at us and said something in French. I supposed he wanted our order. I pointed to Bob. They spoke, and the waiter left.

"What are we having for supper, Bob?"

"Poulet avec something, I think."

Our meals arrived. We ate like two hungry wolves. I'm still not sure what it was, but it was real tasty. The French sure know how to cook.

Relaxing over a coffee and a tiny glass of sweet, strong liquor—Bob called it a *digestif*— I noticed a couple of noses pressed against the windows.

"Look Bob! Two fellows peering in, just like we did an hour ago. They can't afford rich food like this, I suppose."

"Let them eat cake," Bob sniffed.

"The last one to say that lost her head."

The bill arrived. Mon Dieu! Beans for dinner tomorrow—*avec* cake. Even so, we slept well in our pup tent that night.

Bob, somewhere in France.

Bob convinced me to go to the opera with him. He seemed to be somewhat knowledgeable about this type of cultural experience, but I was completely ignorant. Well, I had heard of *Madame Butterfly*, but that was it. I figured opera was just a bunch of fat Italians screeching at each other.

But I agreed to go. We were in Europe, after all. And so, in our anoraks and boots we attended the opera.

Despite myself, I started to enjoy the performance. I didn't understand the words or the story, but there was something about the music and the passion of the singers that stirred me. The audience was enthralled, and I was beginning to get carried away.

Then I heard a snore. To my horror, it was Bob. I elbowed him in the ribs and he woke with a start. For a minute or two. Then he was off, louder again, a real bucksaw.

Another dig. He lasted five minutes this time. Then his head dropped. *Zzzzzzzzzzz.* "Bob," I whispered, "wake up." My cultural mentor was embarrassing me amidst the glitterati of southern Europe.

Then, thank heavens, the opera was over. The audience went wild, hooting and whistling and shouting "on core." This snapped Bob out of his slumber and he joined in, making as much noise as anyone. So ended my first and only opera.

In Sete we also visited a library, because Bob the navigator wanted to check out our route. The librarian, to our amazement, invited us to dinner the next night. We donned our cleanest dirty shirts (as Johnny Cash would later sing) and cycled to her home.

A scrumptious home-cooked French meal, our first home-cooked meal in months. It was a magnificent treat and a wonderful thing to do. The lady's name was Madame Montgolfier. She served soup (not sure what kind), purée (potato, garlic, milk, cheese), ham, anchovies dipped in olive oil, French bread, wine, soft dessert pudding, biscuits, and spirits (which were too strong to drink, we had to suck them through sugar cubes). It was the first time Bob and I had seen artichokes—they looked like green pine cones. Madame Montgolfier had to show us how to eat them.

Bob suggested we follow the Canal du Midi toward Carcassonne and then cross the Pyrenees mountains to Spain. On our bikes!

I made a sketch of Bob and a mongrel we befriended. He was writing home to his Mom in Nova Scotia (Bob was writing, not the dog).

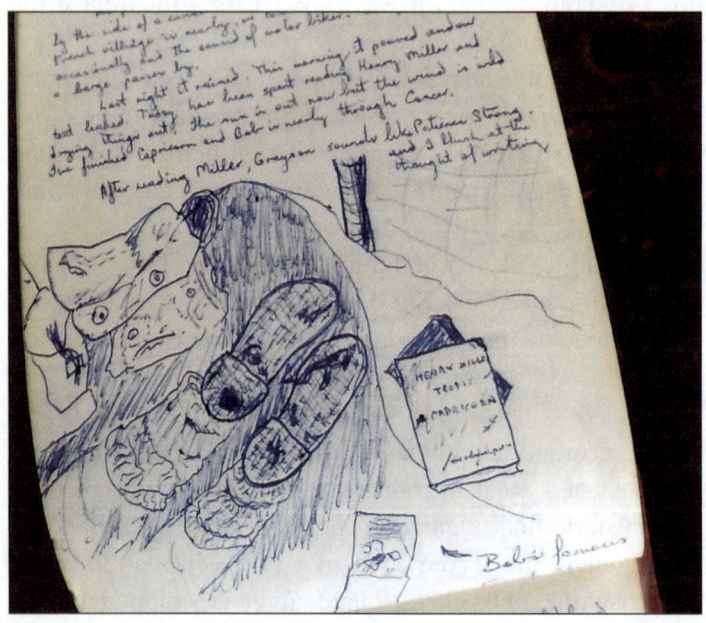

Our next meal wasn't nearly as satisfying as the one Madame Montgolfier had prepared. We'd pitched our tent on the banks of the Canal du Midi, the famous waterway built hundreds of years ago from the Mediterranean to the Atlantic coast. It cut off the long and hazardous sea voyage around Spain and Portugal, where bloodthirsty English pirates had prowled the coast (my ancestors, perhaps).

Once a busy place, the canal at the time of our visit carried mostly tourists and a few barges. Every now and then we heard a boat pass by as we prepared supper.

"No coffee left," said Bob, the designated chef for the evening. "How about running back to that little store we passed? They'll think you're a Frenchman!" He grinned.

Off I went, 5 miles or so, under a threatening sky. "Wee monsieur, comma sa va?" greeted the shopkeeper, who was wearing a beret.

"Coffee, silver plates," I replied.

"Wee wee," he responded.

That means *yes*. I smiled to myself, proud of my newly acquired linguistic skills. At least he understood me.

I paid the French grocer and left with my neatly bundled package. As I cycled down the village road and into the countryside, the skies opened up and the rain began to pelt.

I was soaked as I crawled into our pup tent.

"Ah, great," said Bob. "Nothing like a hot cup of coffee on a day like this."

He opened the soggy bag.

It wasn't instant coffee. It was coffee beans!

We burst into laughter. So much for my French.

And so, with the wind howling and the rain pounding on the thin canvas of our tent, we hammered away at the coffee beans in the frying pan, trying to grind them into a rough powder.

Later, with steaming mugs of lumpy tar, Bob looked up "instant" in his French dictionary.

What a night it turned into! The tent nearly blew down. We had to crawl out of our sleeping bags and try to pin down the flimsy canvas as a fine mist drenched us. I guess the storm, if I can call it that, was what they called a *mistral* in that part of the world. A sudden burst of wind and rain that can drive people crazy.

Perhaps we were nuts ourselves, for we burst into laughter as we looked at each other, desperately clinging to the canvas, soaking wet, with the wind howling, threatening to blow us into the Canal Midi.

But the sun came out in the morning. We dried off as best we could and were on our way to Carcassonne. Soggy but happy wanderers. We stopped for a cup of coffee in a café. Bob ordered, just in case.

Who would have thought salt fish in a window would make me homesick?

Carcassonne is a magnificent walled city. It would have been quite a fortress in medieval days; it is said to date to Roman times. Once again, I was astounded by the difference between the old world and the new. Back home, we bragged about a 100-year-old home. Here, 1,000 years is yesterday. Practically all the homes in Newfoundland are built of wood; in France the houses are stone or brick or stucco.

It's another world. No woods, no barrens, no ponds. I saw a salt codfish in the window of a shop yesterday; it made me hungry and slightly homesick.

Bob gazing at the Pyrenees.

We could see the Pyrenees mountains ahead; there was snow on them. People had told us that wolves roamed around them.

Well, we figured, if Don on his motorcycle could brave the boa constrictors of the Amazon, we shouldn't be afraid of a pack of wolves. Should we?

We chickened out. We decided to put our bikes on the train and stop over in a place called La Molina, in the Spanish Pyrenees.

I had very limited knowledge of Spanish, so I became the linguist this time. I wrote this to make sure that the train conductor didn't lose our bicycles:

Señor Conductor
Deseamos visiter Molinas primero por pocoy dias y continuarmos e Barcelona mas tarde. Reclamerous nuestras bicycletas entouces. Quie hora va al tren a Barcelona via Molina.

We gave my note to the conductor. He grinned at my Spanish, I suppose, and waved us aboard. We were off across the mountains. Next stop Spain—or so we thought.

To be honest, I'd never heard of Andorra, but Bob the map reader had and sure enough it was on our route over the Pyrenees, between France and Spain. It's a country about as big, I'd say, as Fogo Island.

And there we were. A very brief station stop. After a while staring out the window at the tiny snow-covered country, Bob said, "I'm going to get off. I want to be able to say I was in Andorra."

"Bob. The train is ready to go any second now!"

But he was already dashing out and I'll be damned if he didn't jump off the train and into a bank of snow. The train started to move. He was stuck fast. Somehow he managed to break loose, grab my hand, and swing aboard. That was close, I tell you.

"Nearly lost my boots," he said with a laugh, as we chugged out of Andorra.

So I nearly entered Spain with a barefooted partner, but at least Bob could brag about being in Andorra for 45 seconds.

And then we *were* in Spain, halfway across the Pyrenees. We had chickened out of cycling partly because of the wolves, but cycling in the snow through the mountains had worried us too. It was our Grand Tour, after all, not an Everest expedition.

We felt silly enough as it was, wheeling our bikes off the train through snowdrifts.

Anyway, there we were, nestled away in a nice *pension* in the mountains of Spain, just 115 pesetas a day for room and board. Nice people, they made us part of the family, even inviting us to a birthday party where the *pension* owner's 14-year-old daughter helped us with our Spanish. She squealed with delight when we feigned horror in learning that a lizard that we had seen on our hike was poisonous.

Looking out the window of our room the next morning I saw a troop of soldiers carrying skis. I took a few pictures. Bob cautioned me, reminding me that we were in Spain, a fascist state. Franco was a buddy of Hitler and Mussolini and he still ruled with an iron fist.

"Don't get us jailed as spies," Bob warned, as I stowed away the film.

Off the mountains and cycling again. We headed

Soldiers in La Molina, Spain. Photo taken from our window.

for Zaragosa, where Bob had the address of Conchita, a friend's pen pal.

We camped out and cooked breakfast. We were warm—we were in sunny Spain.

A troop of professional cyclists whizzed by on their fancy racing bikes. You could almost see question marks over their heads as they glanced at us and our old-fashioned English bicycles laden with our worldly possessions. Cycling gypsies.

Some days we cycled 60 kilometres or so (about 50 miles). We stopped whenever we felt like it. No rush. No panic. Once, choking with thirst, we tried to get a bottle of wine

The Grand Tour

in a village. It was a Spanish holiday; every shop was locked up. We banged on a door, hoping someone would let us in. A man appeared at an open window upstairs and called out to us, wondering what we were up to.

"Vin sil voo ple," cried Bob.

"Bob, we're not in France," I hissed.

"Vino, por favour," I shouted.

The man came down. We got our vino for 10 cents (the Canadian equivalent). Viva Espana!

Later in the day we sat by the side of the road, enjoying some bread and the dregs of the wine, when a tour bus passed us and slowed down. A crowd of white-haired tourists gazed out the windows at us. Was that pity or envy, I wonder?*

We set out to look up the pen pal. We knocked on an apartment door and a little girl appeared. She couldn't have been more than five years old, but she spoke English better than I did Spanish. Our five-year-old interpreter gave us a new address for Conchita.

Finally, we found Conchita. She was delighted to meet us and spoke some English. She introduced us to her friends Josephina and Pili. We were in heaven. Three beautiful Spanish girls to show us around Zaragosa. They even took us to a bullfight.

Josephina worked in a radio station, where we were interviewed (in Spanish). I hadn't fully realized how terrible

---

*Thirty years later, I was a white-haired tourist on a European bus tour myself. Gazing out the window, my mind wandered back to those carefree days of the Grand Tour.

Bob chats with Josephina, Pili, and Conchita in Zaragosa, Spain.

Our new friends take us to a bullfight.

my Spanish was until then. They probably didn't use it on air. I blush to think of it.

Beautiful warm Barcelona. Hard to believe it was February. I thought of Dad and my brother Don. I bet they were shovelling snow, and here we were in shirtsleeves.

Another magnificent city, a huge sprawling exciting place, the capital of Catalan Province. The residents have their own culture and language, though we were told it's suppressed by the French regime. Sometimes people whispered stories to us, not knowing our meagre understanding of Spanish. I wasn't sure what they were talking about—most likely about regional suppression or atrocities committed during the brutal Spanish Civil War. It had been burned in people's memories. Bob told me that many Canadians had fought in that war. I made a note to look it up, to find out if any Newfoundlanders had signed up. I thought of the unprocessed film of the soldiers stowed away in the bottom of my packsack.

But I had a more immediate problem. I had lost my passport. I went to the British Consulate, as there was no official Canadian representative. I was told it was a serious matter, losing a passport, and they informed the police. I was interrogated in Spanish by three detectives, just like in the movies. I was told to stay in Barcelona until the matter was cleared up. A sort of house arrest.

I was worried that this would take up too much time and money. I felt stupid. I hid away the film I had taken of the soldiers.

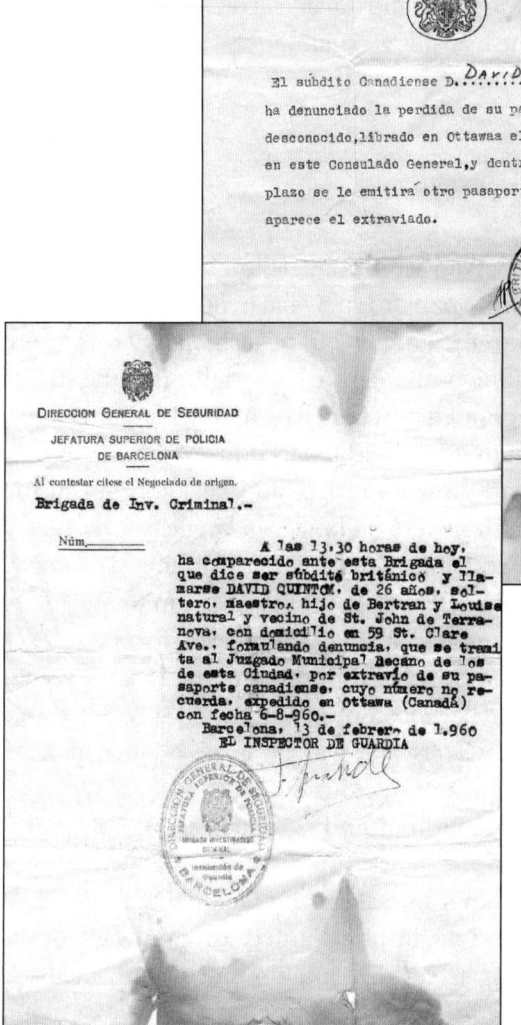

My official documents from the Barcelona police and the British Consulate.

Whoopee! Somebody had found my passport somewhere in Las Ramblas and turned it in to the Barcelona police. Thank heavens! Free again.

And Spanish sailors with bearded lips,
And the beauty and mystery of the ships,
And the magic of the sea.

Lines from Henry Wadsworth Longfellow's "My Lost Youth" had come to mind. Spaniards may have sported beards years ago, but beards were certainly out of fashion when we were in the country. One time we were chased through the streets of Barcelona, hounded by a bunch of urchins pointing at us, jeering and shouting "barbudo, barbudo" ("bearded one"). Bob, you see, had grown a beard, and he stood out in the crowd—bearded lips were no longer in vogue.

It was embarrassing, to say the least. Finally, to get away from the kids, we burst into an undignified run to our bikes, mounted them, and left the little urchins far behind.

El barbudo came back to the hostel the next day with another story. He had been munching on a piece of coconut down by the waterfront, watching the boats, when he was approached by a pushy tour operator.

"A tour of the harbour and coastline, señor, for an unbelievable price?"

Bob declined, but the salesman wouldn't take no for an answer. Again and again he persisted, dropping his price. He was not going to let this gullible tourist with bearded lips escape.

"No. I have no money!" Bob finally shouted.

Exasperated, the salesman threw up his hands and began to walk away. Suddenly he turned on his heel and pointed his finger at Bob.

"You, you, you are an existentialist!"

"Why? What do you mean?" responded Bob.

"You grow a beard, you eat coconuts, and you have no money."

Bob got a great kick out of that definition of existentialism. Maybe it's as good as any.

By the road in Majorca.

Bob and I decided to take a boat to Majorca—a large Spanish island in the Mediterranean. We landed with our bikes in Palma, the island's biggest city. We found a beautiful *pension* decorated in the Moorish style. This island, and much of Spain, was controlled by the Moors from Africa until the 15th century.

The interior of our posh pension in Palma.

We left Palma after several days and headed for the hills. It was mountainous country and, after three days of cycling, we were pooped and wishing we had those 10-speed bikes the pro cyclists were using. We were on the northern coast, moving from one village to another.

We booked into Pension Manuel on a narrow street in the village of Estellience. We were welcomed by our hosts—Manuel and his wife—and a fantastic meal of paella, twin beds, and a balcony overlooking a garden full of orange trees.

Bob, a Guardia Civil, and our pension.

There was a Guardia Civil in this peaceful little village. He walked around in uniform with a nasty looking gun on his shoulder; he seemed completely out of place.

And there was a big mean-looking foreigner in the café. He kept to himself, sipping cognac and watching, watching. We wondered if he was a war criminal in hiding. He could be! Franco had been supported by Mussolini and Hitler.

Bob told me I was getting paranoid—that the foreigner was probably a butterfly collector.

Nevertheless, I thought of my lost passport episode and of the pictures I'd taken of the Spanish soldiers on manoeuvres in the Pyrenees.

We explored Estellience, wandering about the village and checking out a café. Bronzed old fellows were in the café, sipping café solo. It's bitterly strong coffee in a small cup. It was so warm I figured everyone would be having ice cold lemonade or beer. But when in Rome … We downed our café solos. Ugh.

To cool off, Bob and I walked down to the harbour for a swim. We jumped in and were nearly paralyzed. The water was bitterly cold. Must be icebergs in the Mediterranean.

A man saw us swimming and walked away, scratching his head. Bet we were the talk of the town that night. (Bob said the Guardia Civil watched us too. Maybe he thought we were foreign spies.)

That was the day I gave up smoking. It wasn't healthy, I'd heard, and we couldn't really afford the needless expense.

"I'm quitting," I shouted and, with a flourish, threw half a pack of the vile weeds into the Mediterranean.

"Hey, those were my cigarettes!" Bob cried.

For a week we enjoyed the meals and the hospitality of Señor and Señora Manuel and their friends. Manuel serenaded us with his guitar every evening. Full *pension*, including laundry, was about $13 a week. Señora Manuel even sewed up a hole in my pants. I dreaded leaving.

Dave Quinton

Estellience, our village and home for a few weeks.

Bob with Señor and Señora Manuel.

The Grand Tour

Bob and I decided to split up for a few weeks (not because of the cigarettes, mind). I wanted to walk and hitchhike and he wanted to cycle again. We didn't have a fight or anything; we just needed a break from each other.

I hit the road on my own, walking with my packsack on my back.

I headed for Formentor on the northwest corner of Majorca. Decided not to stay there; it was an expensive tourist destination for the rich and famous. And I wasn't either. I just wanted to see it.

Tired of hiking, I stuck out my thumb. An expensive car pulled over. A well-tailored elderly man beckoned me aboard. He spoke to me in German (why do so many people think I'm German?), then he tried French, and then Spanish. Hearing my atrocious Spanish he switched to English. I told him where I was from and where I'd been. He wondered what I thought of Spain, and Majorca in particular.

I praised the place, of course. Then he spied the book I'd been trying to read, by Miguel de Unamuno, a revered writer in Spain but a tough read for me. He was mightily impressed that this foreign vagabond was at least trying to understand his favourite author.

"You are going to Cap de Formentor," he said. "Would you like to spend a few days at my villa?"

Sensing my hesitation, he added, "I am going away on business and will not be there but my servants will take care of you."

So that's how I ended up in a splendid villa on a hill

overlooking the resort of Formentor. Far below were swarms of tourists on a beach, paying through the nose for their holiday. I had two servants to attend to my every need. Cooked meals. A soft bed. A thick carpet. Fruit trees in the garden.

From the balcony of my hacienda I gazed in sympathy at the rich people playing far below. I couldn't wait to tell Bob about my Big Rock Candy Mountain.

Thank you, Señor Villalonga. Thank you, Miguel de Unamuno.

March 1961 already! Three months into the Grand Tour. I had been trudging for an hour or so along the dusty road to Ronda when a little voice piped out, "Hola Engles." I turned to see a bright-eyed boy of about 10 surrounded by 40 or so black and white pigs.

Wearing raggedy grey clothes and short pants, the miniature swineherder also wore a straw sombrero and a huge grin. For some reason he figured out right away I was an Englishman, not a German. I strolled over for a chat.

The sun sizzled. The pigs grunted. And Jose, for that was his name, was eager to learn about this wandering Engles Marinero. Why he thought I was a sailor, I don't know. But he was so enthralled with the idea that I accepted the occupation.

I didn't know enough Spanish to really converse, but with sign language and laughter we managed. We talked of school, of cowboys, of ships, and of his life all day in the fields tending pigs. Every now and then Jose would jump up

Jose and his charges.

to chase squealing piglets from the bushes.

I asked him why there was a hole in the top of his straw sombrero and he explained that one day when he was asleep in the field a hungry pig wandered over and had a feast. We both had a laugh over that.

I hated to leave this vivacious little fellow and his grunting charges, but it was time to go. The road was long and there was a mountain at the end of it. So I took a photo of Jose and his pigs and waved goodbye.

"Adios, Jose."

"Adio, Dawveed."

The mountain wasn't very high, 520 metres or about 1,600 feet. About half as high as Gros Morne, I figured. It even had a road leading to the summit. And on the summit, a monastery.

I decided I wanted to climb instead of walk up the road. I don't remember why—maybe I just wanted to hike through some wild country.

I found a trail that must have been a sheep or goat track because it wandered all over the place, back and down the hill, so I finally had to pick my way up among the bushes. No trees. I wondered if there were snakes.

Hot, hot, hot. I flopped down to munch on a chocolate bar and squeeze the last drop of wine from my goatskin. I hoped that the monks made wine and that they welcomed thirsty wanderers.

Then I saw a sheep's bell on the ground. I'd been hearing

My souvenir sheep's bell.

the distant tinkling of these bells all over Majorca. A great souvenir.

With 500 or so feet to go I wished I had a Sherpa to give me a spell with this packsack.

Then, there it was, the monastery—at least I supposed it was. I was standing in front of a stone wall that I couldn't see over. I thought about climbing it—but what if the monks carried shotguns? I followed the wall around the crest of the hill and eventually came to the monastery entrance.

To my surprise, the first person I met was an elderly lady. She kept a bar/restaurant for thirsty pilgrims and, after I quenched my thirst, she ushered me into the monastery.

"Yes," said the monk whose name was Father (or was it Brother?) Raphael, "you may stay here for the night. You are Canadian, so you speak English—and Spanish?"

"Un pocito," I responded, using about 10 per cent of my Spanish vocabulary in that sentence and silently praying that the holy man would continue in English.

Perhaps reading the panic in my face, he did, and proceeded to tell me about the place as he showed me through the monastery. He told me that the monastery was where the great Father Raimon had lived in the 14th century. Had I heard of him?

Miraculously, I had, from my reading about the history of Majorca. Father Raimon had written hundreds of books about science as well as religion. He had enjoyed a wild youth and startling love affair before being inspired in this monastery to devote his life to God and learning. He died in

Majorca, Spain.

Africa trying to convert the Moslems to Christianity.

Father Raphael was greatly pleased that this young foreigner had heard of the great man. He introduced me to Friar Juan. The spitting image of Friar Tuck he was! Friar Juan spoke to me in Spanish and soon both monks knew just how *pocito* my knowledge of their language was.

Friar Juan showed me to my room—or was it a cell? He opened the window to let in a flood of light and warm air. He bade me *buenos noches*.

So there I was, hove off in a monastery on a mountaintop in Majorca, trying to go to sleep. No television. No radio. Not a sound except for the scratching of my ballpoint pen as I wrote in my journal and the fluttering of a moth about the light bulb.

Be quiet, moth. You're not supposed to dance in a monastery.

Late the next morning I thanked the monks and left. I took the road this time and stopped to have a bite to eat. Perched on a rock just off the road, I was munching on a piece of bread when I heard chanting in the distance. It was English, and eerie.

Male voices chanting English with a Spanish accent? It grew louder and louder. I thought I was losing my mind. Then around a bend in the road they appeared, a crowd of young monks marching and chanting …

"Zee doc ran after ze cat."

"Ze bread will bak in zee oh-veen."

"We are stewdents of Eenglis."

They were indeed. Their instructor led the group like a drum major. They passed below me on my perch, and they didn't even see me. I was tempted to speak, but I was too shy.

Maybe I could have gotten a job with the monks as an English teacher.

An old beggar lady with a little girl in tow approached me as I was waiting for a train. I gave her a few coins. Later I saw them sitting on the ground counting their meagre profits for the day. The old lady's legs were covered in sores. She was ancient.

Suddenly the little girl jumped up, came to me, and, with a smile, presented me with a tiny picture of a holy

Bob in a Spanish village, neither of us are exactly sure where.

woman in blue. Her name, printed under the picture, was Nuestra Señora de Candelaria.

Our Lady of Candelaria. The Virgin Mary, I supposed. A thank you from a beggar and a little girl. (I learned later that Our Lady of Candelaria is the patron saint of the Canary Island—in the North Atlantic—and yet the old lady was in Majorca, in the Mediterranean. Strange. I guess saints have wings like angels. Or double jurisdictions.)

Later, I had a meal with some gypsies, at least I supposed they were gypsies. Dark-skinned and wearing big earrings, they sat across the table from me in a cheap cheap restaurant.

I feasted on a steak for a few pesetas. I think it was a steak, though maybe not from a cow.

Bob and I were re-united. With much laughter we exchanged stories of our adventures over the previous two weeks. He'd stayed in Estellience for a few days after I'd left. He told me about the day television came to the village.

Everyone in the village had gathered in a hall for the big event. A monitor had been set up, and Bob had joined the crowd for the countdown.

Silence. All eyes riveted on the monitor. A test pattern appeared on the screen.

A cheer from the audience—television!

A loud bang, a puff of smoke from the monitor, and it was all over. It was brief, but television had come to Estellience ... with a bang.

It dawned on us that, with the exception of my Formentor benefactor, neither of us had heard any English for a long time. Well, Jose the boy with the pigs had a few words, I suppose, but that was pidgin English blended with pidgin Spanish and sign language. Oh yes, and the monks. But that was it.

It was hot. Must have been 90 degrees. Bob and I spotted an ice cream stand doing a booming business, and we decided to treat ourselves to ice cream. While we waited in the long lineup, we chatted away, in our native tongue, of course.

"Dos por favour," I proudly said—to impress Bob, I suppose, or maybe to impress the young lady who was serving the ice cream.

As she filled the cones, she nonchalantly asked, "Where you guys from?"

"Er—Canada," I blurted.

"What part?"

Bob and I answered in unison: "Nova Scotia—Newfoundland."

"What part of Newfoundland?"

"St. John's"

"What part of St. John's?"

"West end. St. Clare Avenue."

"I was born on Morris Avenue," she declared. Morris Avenue is off St. Clare. We must have been neighbours. I'd probably gone to school with her.

She was busy with customers and I was too stunned to ask any intelligent questions but I gathered from the hurried conversation that she had married or her mother had married a Spaniard visiting Newfoundland to buy salt fish. She'd been in Spain for some time. I didn't even copy down her name.

As they still say—wherever you go, you'll find a Newfoundlander. (Seven months on our Grand Tour and the only Canadian we meet is a Newfoundlander. You talk about!)

I desperately needed a new pair of pants. I found a pair of "absolutely top quality, made in Italy, less than half price," the vendor said. Obviously, the deal of a lifetime.

I bought them. A few hours later, hitching a ride, I jumped aboard the back of a truck and ripped them from stem to stern. Came completely apart at the seams. Bob laughed his head off.

Bob as Mark Antony.

We came upon the ruins of what we figured was a Roman amphitheatre—crumbling stone seats encircling an area where, I supposed, the Christians had battled the lions. Or maybe it was a theatre where plays had been performed 2,000 years or more ago.

"Let's put some life in the place before you take a picture," said Bob, who had cycled back to our *pension* and returned with a bedsheet.

Minutes later, in his hastily assembled toga, Bob made a credible Mark Antony and struck a heroic pose that would have made Shakespeare proud.

"Friends, Romans, countrymen—lend me your ears," he shouted. "I come to bury Caesar not to …"

Just then a group of tourists appeared and gazed in

stunned silence as a red-faced Mark Antony and his scribe scrambled aboard their chariots and cycled madly away. So ended Bob's brief career as a Shakespearean actor. How we laughed at our foolishness.

April. Time to talk finances. We'd been on the road nearly four months and our cash was getting low. We doubted that we'd find jobs in Spain, so we planned to scoot back to England as fast as we could. Surely we'd find jobs there.

From the window of our train (note steam), leaving Spain.

Chapter 4 • England, Part 2
The Grand Tour

We leapfrog. Bikes and trains and the ferry across the Channel and we were back in England. It was spring and, though not hot, it was quite pleasant. And it was indeed good to be there. The only problem was that I was flat broke and living off Bob, who had precious little himself.

We (I should say *he*) rented an apartment in Earls Court from a Polish couple (refugees from the war, I think) and we both began to hunt for jobs. Not as easy as one might think. We checked the newspapers and applied, but we weren't really suitable or, I suspect, suitably attired. Also, no references ... and no useful skills.

Eventually Bob landed a job packing and delivering lunches to schools. He got to ride around London in a lorry, though he couldn't understand a word the Cockney driver said.

I got nothing. Bob was great about it but I hated sponging off my old friend. He was barely paying the rent. A beer

and a pork pie was a luxury. Maybe tomorrow …
Nothing. Nothing. Nothing.

I discovered an ad for a store that bought used clothing. East End Misfits. I crossed London on the tube (subway) with my skates and blue overcoat, my prized possessions I had stored in London while we had travelled to Spain.

I got £1 for my skates. I was sad to part with them, but I had to eat.

My overcoat fetched £2. Not bad, I thought. Nice to have some coins to jangle in my pocket.

An Australian seaman who'd been looking at a rack of coats while I made my deal followed me outside and offered me twice what I'd got for my overcoat if I could get it back. He figured the old fellow inside would charge him a fortune. It was a good coat and he was about my size.

I considered his proposition for a moment, told him to wait around the corner, and went back inside with a cock and bull story about going to northern Scotland and reconsidering. It was cold there. Maybe I'd be better off pawning my new Harris tweed jacket instead. I said I'd run home and get it if he would give me back my overcoat.

His eyes lit up. I gave him the £2, he gave me back my overcoat. I scooted around the corner. The Aussie tried it on. Perfect fit. He gave me £4. Doubled my profit.

£4. About $15. I was rich.

I was, I admit, bored. And lonely. Not much to write in my notebooks. I needed to socialize. I read in a paper there was an old-time dance in a hall. Having learned to dance the Lancers in Trepassey years before and having been to many a square set in Red Cliff, I donned my plaid shirt and dancing shoes and found the place.

Hearing music, I peered in the window. A crowd was dancing, but of course it wasn't a set or the Lancers. Dressed in tuxedos and fancy dresses they were gracefully twirling around to 18th-century minuets or something.

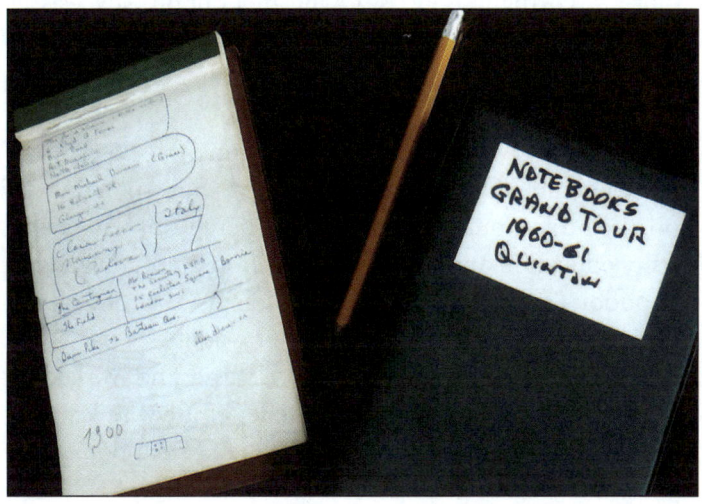

Disappointed, I slunk off home. The Grand Tour had gone sour.

I went to the Tate Gallery to impress my artist friend Gary back home.

While gazing at the paintings I saw a stunningly beautiful girl enter the room. How could I meet her?

I devised a strategy. She was moving right to left. I moved left to right, just fast enough to be, by coincidence, next to her as she gazed at the scene of a fierce battle. My chance. I laughed. She looked at me.

"Do you know why I laughed?" I asked. "I just saw a painting like this in France and the English soldiers were ugly. Here the French are the bad guys."

It was a lie but it worked, and we struck up a conversation. A Portuguese girl studying in London, she was as lonely as I was. We became good friends.

Thanks for getting me to go to the Tate, Gary.

Broke again. Overcoat gone. Skates gone. Hockey career over. England's Olympic hopes dashed. Still sponging off Bob, the professional orange peeler. There I was with a university education and unable to find a job—not much work in London for a forester or wildlife biologist. I wrote a letter to Kenya National Parks, maybe their wildlife service could use someone like me ... I've trapped beaver and worked on caribou ... Nah, hopeless. I sent the letter anyway.

I decided to ask Bob if he could get me an appointment as an assistant orange peeler.

INCREDIBLE! I finally landed a job.

While I was walking through Hyde Park, I saw a young man picking up branches that had fallen off trees and putting them in a bag. I asked him how he got his job. He pointed to a building. I went there and told a receptionist that I was looking for work. Any kind of work.

She excused herself, entered an office, spoke with some people, came back and told me to wait. She resumed typing. Every now and then a head would appear and gaze at me for a moment. I was being appraised, I guessed. Jeez, I only want to pick up sticks.

The receptionist was beckoned into the office and soon returned.

"Yes, we have a position for you," she said as she handed me some forms. "We have an opening for a labourer on the gardening staff of Buckingham Palace."

I must have muttered *huh?* or some other intelligent remark, so she explained that the office I was in hired for all the parks in London, including the Royal Gardens. I was to report there the next day at precisely 7 a.m.

I went home to our apartment in a daze and told Bob. He burst into hysterical laughter.

"Don't laugh! You can call me Lord David now, you mere professional orange peeler!" I was delighted, and scared, and I didn't sleep a wink. Me, on the gardening staff of Buckingham Palace.

I didn't want to disappoint Her Majesty by being late, so I boarded the tube quite early. I wore my best working clothes and army surplus boots. On each side of me sat rather stiff, sour-looking gentlemen with bowler hats and umbrellas. I badly wanted to say to them: "And where do you work, old chaps?" If they responded, I would tell them about my place of employment: *Buckingham Palace.*

The gardening staff entrance was a little door in the

wall that was opened by an old fellow with a hunchback who arrived on bicycle at precisely 6:59. His key entered the lock precisely at 7 a.m. and five or six of us workmen paraded in.

We were met by the head gardener, Mr. Bob Nutbeam, a middle-aged gentleman who welcomed me. I was put to work watering flowers and planting tulips in the most magnificent setting imaginable.

Behind Buckingham Palace lies a magnificent walled, park-like garden of about 47 acres. Essentially, it's the backyard of the kings and queens of Britain.

I felt like I was in a dream. I was watering the huge stone vases beneath the Royal bedchamber—I bet I was the first Newfoundlander to do that! Then, planting and weeding.

The staff were nice and friendly, mostly about my age. Not a bit stiff or formal. In fact, there was plenty of good-natured horsing around when we were behind the bushes and Mr. Nutbeam couldn't see us.

We had to be careful though. The Royal Family often came out for a stroll. Wouldn't want to feel the wrath of the monarchy by doing anything foolish.

Hadn't seen any of the Royal Family yet. But still—what a job. I couldn't believe it.

The lawn in the Royal Gardens is immense. The old fellow with the hunchback who opened the door in the palace wall in the morning drove a motorized lawn cutter—a neat rig I'd never seen at home. (Well, maybe they had one at Bally Haly.) It looked like fun. I wished he'd give me a turn, but I guess it's fair that we younger guys get all the grunt work.

Saw Prince Charles striding across the lawn. He must have been about 12 or 13. There was a pond in the Royal Gardens which a flock of flamingoes call home. They're tropical birds and I wondered how they survived the winter ... but then I was told that they'd just arrived. The birds hadn't yet spent a winter in England.

I hoped the pond wouldn't freeze. With their skinny legs they'd be in trouble.

The fellows on the gardening staff were horsing around, teasing a bobby at the gate about physical fitness and showing off, bragging about the judo belts they had. They brought me into the conversation.

"David, do you have any belts?"

"Oh yeah," I lied, not wanting the boys to think I was a pansy.

"What colour?"

I was trapped. I took a chance.

"Black," I said, nonchalantly.

They backed off, impressed. No horsing around after that.

I'd made a good choice. I couldn't fight my way out of a wet paper bag! My black belt held up my pants.

Her Majesty Queen Elizabeth has a birch broom. At least she did, until I threw it over the palace walls.

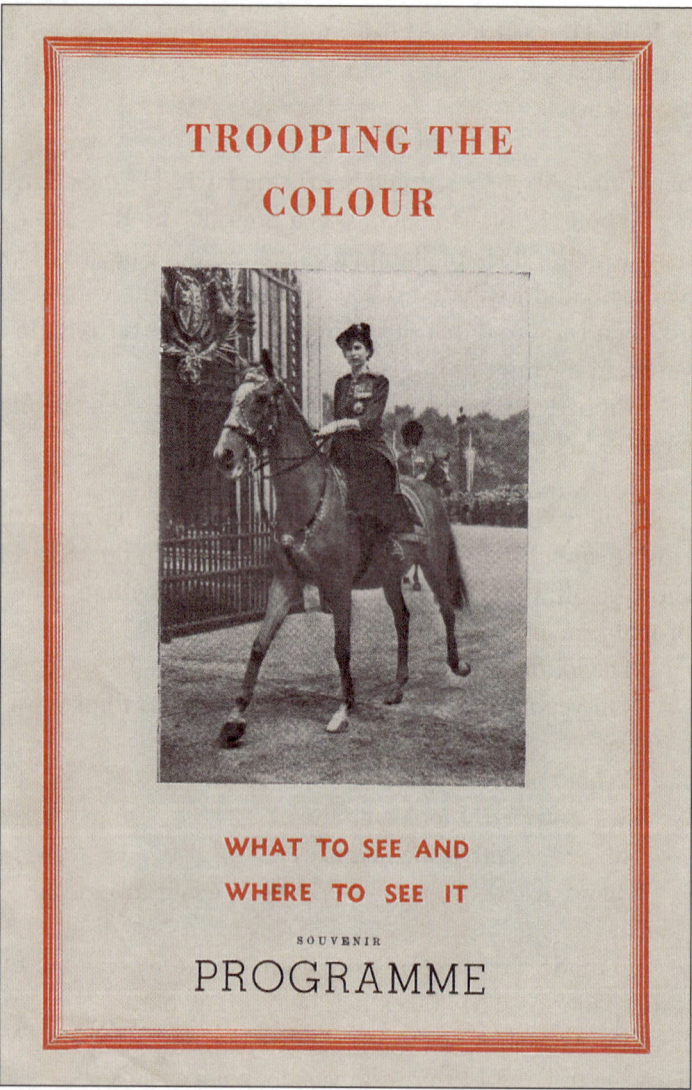

The fellows at work asked if I knew how to play cricket. I didn't, of course, but I said I was a pretty good hand at baseball and decided I'd show them. We were on a shady lane near the wall. Nobody could see us.

My bat was the old-fashioned birch broom that we used to sweep the trails. I stepped up to the plate. I got one of the fellows to pitch me an old tennis ball he'd found. A mighty swing and I hit the ball. As I did, the bundle of birch twigs came off the handle and flew over the palace wall. We scattered.

I wondered what the pedestrians outside thought was going on. Were the Queen and Prince Philip having a racket? Sorry about your broom, Your Majesty.

There was always something of interest in my place of employment, the Royal Gardens of Buckingham Palace (I still loved repeating that). Brian, my best friend on the gardening staff, and I watched Mr. Nutbeam out trying to shoot the rooks that nest in the tall trees and pick off the ducklings as they followed their mother across the lawn to the bobby at the gate. The bobby would stop traffic and squire them across to St. James Park. It was a daily outing for the Royal ducklings, but it also was a hazardous waddle.

Old Nutty, as Brian called him, crept with a shotgun as close as he could to the rooks (they looked like crows to me). Bang. Bang. Didn't touch a feather. The boys said he never could hit one. But just imagine: in Buckingham Palace, in the heart of London. A crow hunt.

Brian told me about an incident he'd had, about a year

before I joined the gardening staff. He had been all along, walking down a path in the gardens. Nobody was around so he began to bang a stick on his empty bucket as he sang the latest rock song.

Rounding a turn in the path he got the surprise of his life. There was the Queen, out inspecting a flower bed.

Terrified, Brian dropped the bucket, ran, and hid behind some bushes. When his heartbeat slowed down he peeped out, figuring he'd lose his job, if not his head. Queen Elizabeth was smiling.

I was finally able to contribute to the rent. It was good feeling. My salary was £8.50 a week. About $23.

Since the failure of the crow hunt I have a new job. I must escort the family of ducks across the lawn to the bobby on duty. London traffic is halted so that they can waddle over to the waters of St. James Park.

Ten years from now I won't believe this, I thought. *Bodyguard to the Royal ducklings.*

I worked at the tulip bed one day, with Prince Andrew nearby in his pram. As nobody was around, we exchanged some baby talk. I wondered if he'd have a Newfoundland accent when he grew up.

One Saturday I visited the Kensington Natural History Museum. I took notes and made sketches of the remarkable displays. I would have loved to work in a museum. We sure didn't have anything like that at home.

I overheard a group of little cockney boys, on a school trip I suppose.

"Oi, look 'ere" (reading the sign), "a Genuine Pig" (guinea pig).

And at the display of ancient skulls: "Oi. This bloke's got rotten toith."

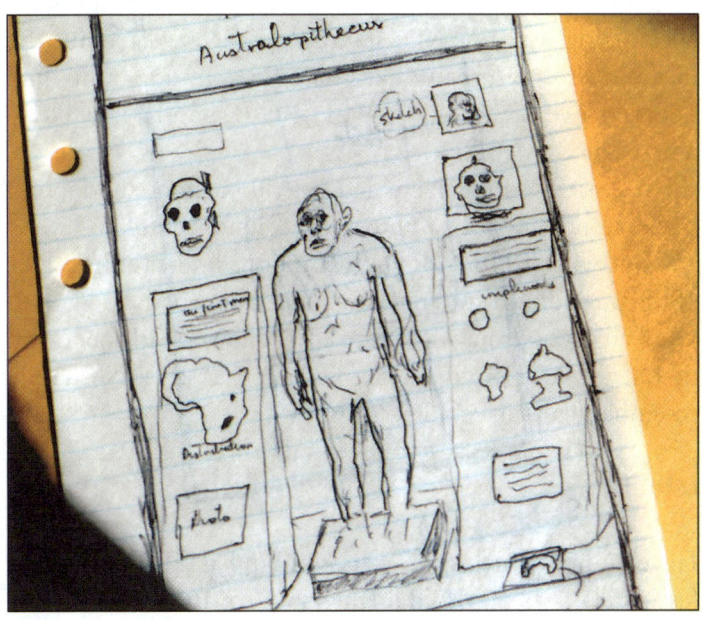

Almost half a year in Europe and I hadn't yet visited the West Country where my ancestors came from. So I decided one weekend to hitchhike there. I didn't really know where they had lived, but I knew there was a good chance they had sailed out of Poole in Dorset.

A young man on a motorcycle picked me up. He was a German, living in London. I climbed on and away we roared. I thought of Lawrence of Arabia, who was killed on a motorcycle around here. And Don Poynter came in mind too. I wondered where he was and wished he could see me now.

My new friend, Conrad, dropped me off in Poole. After exchanging addresses, he sped off and I gazed about the place where my great-great-great-great-grandparents had boarded a vessel bound for Bonavista Bay and a new life in a new land.

It started to rain. I scurried to a phone booth and found a telephone directory. Quite a few Quintons listed.

But what to do? Phone at random and say that their 18th cousin, five times removed, was in town?

I chickened out and went to a pub instead for a pint of bitter and a pork pie. Studied the pubsters. No family resemblance that I could see.

Oh well—at least I could say that I had visited the ancestral homeland.

Have you ever picked up cigarette butts all day long? Professionally, I mean. I did at Buckingham Palace. The Garden Party over, it was our job to pick up the butts left by the guests. A lot of smokers had been there, for sure.

We labourers lined up with military precision and, like a squad of sappers combing a minefield, advanced carefully. A Marlborough here, a Camel there, a foreign butt there. The odd one with a lipstick smear. No roll-your-owns, not with this crowd. And so I spent my day as a professional (Royal?) butt-picker-upper. I forgot to count them. Nutty should have put up a prize.

I decided to visit our old boarding house to see what happened to Bluey, the New Zealand sailor we'd befriended five months before. Had he made it back home? Surely someone would know.

He was still in the boarding house, still puffing on his foul-smelling cigarettes, still teasing the cockneys, still poking pennies in the heater, though it was quite warm in England, still dreaming of southern climes and home.

We greeted each other as long-lost vagabonds and compared adventures.

Bluey had found a job on a freighter bound for the south seas. Unfortunately, it stopped at a port of call (in Amsterdam, I think he said), where Bluey got drunk, disappeared for a while, and the ship left without him. Somehow he ended up back in London. He laughed it off and I had to laugh too. The comradery of super tramps. I thought of John Masefield's "Sea Fever":

And all I ask is a merry yarn from a laughing fellow-rover
And quiet sleep and a sweet dream when the long trick's over.

I hope old Bluey made it home eventually.

Attended the Queen's 35th birthday in June. All of us who took care of the Royal Gardens received a pass for the

> **Board of Green Cloth**
>
> ADMIT THE BEARER TO THE FORE COURT
> BUCKINGHAM PALACE
>
> # THE QUEEN'S BIRTHDAY
> SATURDAY, 10th JUNE, 1961
>
> Dress:
> Ladies: Day Dress, with hat.
> Gentlemen: Uniform or Lounge Suit.
>
> **NO CAMERAS ALLOWED**
>
> *Scarbrough*
> Lord Chamberlain.

Changing of the Guard ceremony. We came in our best bib and tucker. I even polished my army boots. I kept the invitation sent to me by Her Majesty, my boss in 1961.

One of the fellows told me that, years ago, some palace bureaucrat had given the labourers' invitations to his friends. When the Queen Mum heard about it, she hit the palace roof. It didn't happen again.

Everyone among the gardening staff loved the Queen Mum. Oh, they joked and poked fun at the Royal Family and head gardener Mr. Nutbeam, yet I think they'd die to protect any of them.

Nutty was a fine fellow. Noting my interest in the plants and trees of the Royal Gardens, he encouraged me to go to college, maybe become a botanist. It was nice of him and I dared not admit I'd already spent years at university. The class system in England was terrible. I was accepted as I was by my friends on the gardening staff. I didn't want them calling me guv'nor or knuckling their forelocks and regarding me as a "right toff." I enjoyed being one of the boys.

Yet I was getting a bit scruffy. After half a year on the road my clothes were quite shabby, even for a common labourer. Now that I was gainfully employed by Her Majesty, it was time for me to obtain a wardrobe in keeping with my new station in life.

A suit? Why not?

Bob suggested I try Savile Row. I'd never heard of it.

Savile Row, my ass! You'd need a mortgage to buy a necktie! BOB!!

Went to Burtons, where they convinced me to order a tailor-made suit. I thought they were making fun of me, but they weren't, and the price they quoted was reasonable. I went for it—just think, my first tailor-made suit.

A skinny old guy with a tape hanging around his neck took my measurements and suggested something in a "houndstooth" (*houndstooth?*). It would be ready in a few days.

The suit was grey. A snug fit, it hugged my body. I felt lean as a greyhound, all right. (The dog, not the bus.) Me, in a tailor-made suit. A right toff I was, after all. Too bad I had thrown away my scarf!

When I get back to Newfoundland, I'll hobnob with the Bally Haly crowd in my houndstooth. I must get a top hat and go to the Ascot Races.

Tally most frightfully ho!

A letter arrived from home with an offer of a job as extension biologist with the Newfoundland Wildlife Division. Dr. John Green was going back to the States and I had been offered his position, but I had to act. It was too good an opportunity to miss.

Time to settle down, I supposed. I'd been away half a year. I should go home, I supposed ... yet, I liked London. It was a big decision.

Bob had a romance blossoming with Sigrid, a German girl and a friend of Conrad, the fellow who had given me the motorcycle ride to Dorset.

I decided to take the job, and wrote a letter of acceptance. I told Bob that I would be leaving and then I had to tell Mr. Nutbeam and the boys. And let Her Majesty know.

I wonder if anyone ever told Mr. Nutbeam that I was the one who had thrown the Queen's birch broom over the palace walls. I'd been living with fear that the *Daily Mirror* would get hold of the story. Maybe it was a good thing that I was leaving the country.

I picked up a new pair of army surplus boots. I had worn the old pair out in the service of Her Majesty. I had planned a last-minute adventure before heading home: hitchhike to Wales and Ireland, then on to Prestwick. I booked my return ticket. I had arrived by boat, but I would return by plane.

My last day at the Palace. I said goodbye to Mr. Nutbeam and the boys. It was a lowly job, I supposed—plucking weeds and watering flowers, picking up cigarette butts and being bodyguard to the Royal ducklings. But I would miss it.

But, it was time to go home. My wanderlust had been quenched, for the time being. A final jaunt now in my new army surplus boots through Wales and Ireland, then home.

Bill Morgan, a Welshman serving with the Royal Navy, was one of the many soldiers and sailors who had visited my home in St. John's during the war. He had returned to Newfoundland when World War II ended to marry my Aunt Jessie. I wanted to visit his family in Port Dinorwic,

The hills of Wales.

Wales. Uncle Bill's sister Nell welcomed me and introduced me to the family.

The kids swarmed about, giggling and asking questions in a foreign language. It was Welsh of course, the ancient Celtic language that's still spoken in the country, especially in the northern regions. The kids seemed to get a kick out of their parents' speaking English—a foreign language to them. Only about 200 miles or so from London.

I stayed there for a few days, walking the Welsh hills with Griff, Bill's stepbrother, a postman. He was curious about Newfoundland. Little did I know then that Griff would, in a few years, immigrate to St. John's, marry, settle down, and learn to sing "I's da B'y" with a strong Welsh accent.

After this taste of Wales I hoofed and hitchhiked and hopped on the ferry to Ireland.

Though my family on both sides are of English descent, I felt quite at home in Ireland. I guess it was my upbringing in Irish St. John's that did it. The faces seemed familiar and, of course, the voices, the words, the accents. And blame the Big Six music store on Water Street and their Irish-Newfoundland radio show too, I suppose, for I had grown up listening to the McNulty Family and others singing about the wild colonial boy and "Ballyjamesduff."

I solved one musical mystery. I had always wondered about the line "on the banks of the shore that flows down by Moon Coin." How does a shore flow? In Ireland I discovered the word is *suir*, a river, pronounced "shore." And it does flow down by Moon Coin. A lovely song and a pretty place.

Somewhere in Ireland on my whirlwind tour.

And it *is* a long way to Tipperary. I know, I walked there along a country road. No traffic, so no ride. I did meet an elderly lady on the road. As she approached, she shouted, "Where ya going?"

I shouted back, "Tipperary!"

"Ah, 'tis a hungry town," she responded. This conversation was repeated until she'd passed me and was on a distant hill hollering the same question, and me roaring back. Had to smile.

I finally made it and had a great feast in the hungry town. I chatted with a bunch of young fellows who'd heard of Newfoundland and were curious about our cultural and historic ties.

The Irish I met were friendly and warm. I hitched a ride with one fellow who was distributing Irish-language books to schools. They were proud of the old Celtic language that my people had tried to destroy, I guess.

Wandered around Dublin, a marvellous city. I chanced upon a church that claimed to have the mummified remains of crusaders and nuns in a crypt beneath it.

For years I'd been fascinated by archaeology and would have loved to visit Egypt or King Tut's tomb. This was as close as I was going to get, I dare say, so I entered St. Michan's Church, where a man with a trouble lamp escorted me down and introduced me to a nun and a few other mummies. One crusader was so tall they had to break his legs to put him in the casket, which had rotted away. Creepy. Creepy. Creepy!

A phone rang upstairs. My guide left me alone in the tomb staring at my 700-year-old acquaintances. He'd passed me the light and I clung to it for dear life, silently praying that there wouldn't be a power failure. I didn't want to be entombed with a nun and a crusader with broken legs, or with anybody, for that matter.

Finally, the guide returned, thank heavens.

Musty old Europe. I guess you were right, Don Poynter. I needed 40 shades of green and a Guinness after that.

A rush now to get to Scotland for a few days, then to the Prestwick airport for the flight home.

A friendly couple picked me up and insisted on a mini

tour. They showed me Robbie Burns's Cottage and I told them that my uncle and many Newfoundlanders had taken military training in the area and others had served as loggers in the war effort. I managed a quick visit to Loch Lomond, where I took pictures. I dearly wished I had had time to see Loch Ness and the monster.

I was being a typical tourist now: a glimpse of Wales, a rush through Ireland, and a frantic dash about Scotland. Too much to absorb!

Spent the night with Aunt Jessie's friend, Grace Durham (née Symonds), and her husband in Glasgow. A war-groom, I guess you could call him, for, like Uncle Bill, he had married a girl from overseas. We chatted about old times.

Loch Lomond, Scotland.

The Grand Tour

On the plane, I stared down at the Atlantic far below. Over. It was over. My Grand Tour had ended. I'd go to work a proper job. Settle down. Forget England, Wales, Scotland, France, and Spain.

Seven months before, it had taken about a week to cross over to Liverpool. I was returning in a few hours—so fast and easy. Yet, it was fun on the old *Nova Scotia*. Hard to believe that seven months before Bob and I had set sail for Europe.

My head was awash with memories, of the places we'd been and the people we'd met. What an experience! Saying goodbye was hard.

Back home, goodbye always meant "see you again." In Europe, for me, goodbyes meant forever. That made me sad. The people I'd met overseas I'd never see again.

Yet, I was excited about going home. Family. Old friends, new friends, new job, new life.

The pilot announced we'd soon be in Gander. From there I would catch an EPA flight to St. John's. There was land below, the north side of Bonavista Bay. The red light told us to buckle up. I was home. I wondered if Don Poynter had made it to Patagonia.

At St. John's airport I found a dime in my wallet. I phoned Dad to come pick me up. Home! Hugs and kisses. Salt fish, blue potatoes from Red Cliff—dry and fluffy.

"Best potatoes in the world," bragged Dad, as always. And he was right.

Oh yes. And scrunchions. I was home.

Epilogue

1978: Her Majesty the Queen visits Newfoundland

My wife, Françoise—who, incidentally, is a French royalist—and I took our youngest daughter, Christine, to the royal walkabout in Pleasantville.

It was a beautiful day. Christine was all dressed up, of course, and waving her Union Jack. Françoise made sure she was squeezed in front of a cheering crowd. As Her Majesty came by, smiling and chatting with the kids, Françoise nudged me and said, "David, speak with her! Tell her that you worked in the palace, that you watered the flowers under her window. Go on, GO ON!"

I couldn't. I just stood there with a goofy grin, waving my Union Jack, till the moment passed.

Christine was delighted. The Queen had smiled at her! Françoise was less than impressed. I'd blown an opportunity

While we were tourists in London in 2014, Françoise took this picture of me by what was, I believe, the gardening staff entrance to the palace. It's boarded up now. No plaque to commemorate the Canadian cigarette-butt-picker-upper of 1961.

to chat with her Majesty.

I was left feeling nostalgic. I would have liked to ask about old Nutty and the Royal ducklings and apologize for throwing her broom over the Royal garden wall.

I think I'll send her a copy of this book.

In case you were wondering: my first job with the Department of Mines and Resources was fighting the forest fires that swept over Newfoundland in the summer of 1961. Three years later I married Françoise Nicolas of St. Pierre, joined the CBC, and helped pioneer a television program called *Land & Sea*.

Meanwhile, in Europe, Bob married Sigrid, taught school for a while in England, became a bartender in Germany, and moved back to Canada to work with Parks Canada as a naturalist/interpreter. Bob continued to explore the world on foot, hiking about Nova Scotia primarily, but he had one especially memorable time wandering through the mountains of Corsica.

I satisfied my wanderlust mainly by travelling around Newfoundland and Labrador for *Land & Sea*.

Bob and I made one more expedition together. Back in the late 1960s we climbed the Long Range Mountains on Newfoundland's west coast and spent a week exploring the high country back of Bonne Bay. In our 80s now, we keep in touch by letter and phone, reliving our adventures. We laugh a lot.